THE EARLY RETIREMENT HANDBOOK

How to Get There and How to Thrive in the Next Chapter of Your Life

JOHN KAIL

Published by
Thinking Trail Press

The author and publisher have made every effort to ensure that the information in this book was accurate at the time of publication. The content is provided for general educational and informational purposes only and should not be considered financial, investment, tax, or legal advice.

This book is published internationally in English language edition by Thinking Trail Press.

First Edition

ISBN: 979-8-9954905-1-7 (paperback)
ISBN: 979-8-9954905-2-4 (hardcover)
Library of Congress Control Number: 2026918364

For information about permissions, subsidiary rights, or special sales, contact: Thinking Trail Press and the Author.

Published by

Thinking Trail Press

For Anyone dreaming about retirement…

Contents

THE EARLY RETIREMENT HANDBOOK

How to Get There and How to Thrive in the Next Chapter of Your Life

JOHN KAIL

"401(k)s were a part of a larger cultural drift in America away from shared responsibilities toward a more precarious individualism … At one time, there was a social contract that if you played by the rules (went to school, got a job, and worked hard), everything would be fine. That's no longer true today. You can do everything right, just the way society wants you to do it, and still end up broke, alone, and homeless."

Jessica Bruder — *Nomadland: Surviving America in the Twenty-First Century*

PART I: ACHIEVING FINANCIAL FREEDOM

INTRODUCTION

There's nothing special about me. I started my career making $35,000 per year in a job that I was extremely fortunate to get. Nineteen years later, I reached financial freedom and officially left the workforce at the age of forty-two. Whenever anyone finds out that I'm retired, they generally ask the same two questions:

1) How did you do it? and

2) What do you do now?

These questions aren't about me, personally. People generally ask because they want to know how it would apply to their own lives. The purpose of this book is to answer both of these questions. I'm not a CFP. I'm not a CPA. I'm just a guy with a process. Simply put, if I can do it, so can you.

This book is divided into two parts:

1) Achieving financial freedom and

2) Life after early retirement.

I wrote this book from a coaching perspective. I want you to succeed. Most people will never reach financial freedom because they don't believe that they can do it, and they don't know how to get there. Some will reach early retirement but struggle because they knew what they were retiring from, but could never answer what they are retiring to. This book isn't about getting rich; it's about living your best life. It is designed to help you reach success, no matter where you are on your journey.

What is Financial Freedom?

There are varying definitions, but for the purposes of this book, financial freedom is the point when a person has sufficient assets to cover their living expenses. This is also referred to as financial independence. When someone reaches this milestone, work becomes optional. It is an exhilarating state, but it is important to note that it will not solve all of your problems. After basic necessities, money is just a tool to help you live the lifestyle that you want.

What is the Lifestyle that you want?

Look at that, we're not even in the first chapter, and I've already got you thinking. Good. My goal throughout this book is to make you stop, think, and define what this means for your life. Don't worry about answering this for now. We'll come back to it.

Why should you strive for Financial Freedom?

Unfortunately, money is one area of life in which you are forced to participate, whether you like it or not. The good news is that it is not an all-or-nothing venture! It may seem like an impossible goal, but that's okay. The important thing is to start as soon as you can. It doesn't matter what you do or how old you are; it's never too late to start. If you're young, you have the advantage of time. If you're older, you have the advantage of a higher income.

Our financial goal is to be free to live our lives without having to rely on income from a job. Financial freedom is the final boss on your financial journey. Still, there are many important levels that you'll hit along the way. The closer you make it on your path to this milestone, the greater your options will be to live life on your terms. Before I begin a project, I always try to imagine "what happens if this actually works and becomes a smashing success?" Well, success in this realm is financial freedom.

Why Retire Early?

Yes, it takes money to reach our goal, but the end goal is not just money. Our money has a purpose. It is bigger than simply not working. I probably don't need to convince you to pursue early retirement, but here are a few benefits:

Freedom and Control. Your job has control of both your time and your energy. Even when you're not working, you'll find that you are thinking about your job or are too physically or emotionally drained to pursue your interests. You may be physically present with your friends and family, but mentally absent. You can be free from this control.

Health. The first thing you'll notice after retirement is the absence of work-related stress. It is like a mountain of stress has instantly been eliminated from your shoulders. Most people will carry this stress for the majority of their entire lives, damaging the health of both their bodies and their minds. In addition, control of your time and energy allows you to focus on healthier habits and nutrition.

Security and Options. High-paying, creatively fulfilling jobs are exceedingly rare. Even if you do love your job, you may not be able to work as long as you hope. Companies go out of business, technologies change, and jobs are created and destroyed. Financial freedom gives you security in case something does happen. It provides you with the option of working on whichever projects you desire. You don't have control over your employment. Luckily, you do have a lot of control over your finances.

CHAPTER 1
YOU ARE THE CAPTAIN OF YOUR FINANCIAL SHIP

Please say it again with me. You are the one who will ultimately determine your success in this financial endeavor. I like to think of it like the captain of a ship. There will be rough seas. There will be dark nights when it is hard to find your way. There will be strong winds that try to fling you off course or feel like they are blowing directly in your face. Through it all, what's most important and what will keep you on your path is to stay focused on your North Star: financial freedom.

The good news is that there are also periods of strong tailwinds where the massive leaps don't even seem to make mathematical sense. Additionally, although you are the captain of the ship, many different resources can help you along the way. Always continue to educate yourself and do not think that you are alone on this path. Think of this book as an extra rower, always there to help give you a boost on your voyage.

Ok, I'm a little intimidated. Is this even worth it?

My apologies, I can come off as a bit intense at times. I strongly believe that this subject is incredibly important and can change people's lives. The truth is that you may already be doing a lot of the things that I'm going to discuss, and it may not require difficult changes to your life. The first step is always the most important, and the fact that you are reading this means that you are interested and on your way.

In fact, my grand hope through all of this is that you'll achieve something far greater than financial freedom.

CHAPTER 2
YOUR FINANCIAL MACHINE

That's really what this is. You are going to build a machine, and it is going to run 24 hours a day, 365 days a year. After a certain point, your machine will be doing all of the hard work, not you. It will take more of your effort at the beginning to grow the machine, but this thing is going to get to a point where it will carry you for the rest of your life.

Step One – Determine your Net Worth

Hey, finally some actual substance! Alright, I hear ya. Determining your net worth is critically important because it is the scorecard that you are going to be continually tracking for years to come. It is a simple process and will provide critical insight as you progress on your journey. Here's how to do it:

Stop what you're doing and do this now. Open a spreadsheet. The top portion is going to be for Assets (the things you own), the bottom half is going to be for Liabilities (the things you owe). Add a column for each time you update, not more than once per month. I do it every six months. This does not have to be complex! Simply list your accounts and current values. Here's an example of how it looks:

Checking account	$
Savings account	$
Retirement account	$
Car	$

House (if you own)	$
Total Assets (sum of the rows)	$
Mortgage (if you have one)	$
Car loan	$
Student loan	$
Credit card 1	$
Credit card 2	$
Total Liabilities (sum of these rows)	$
Net Worth (Total Assets – Total Liabilities)	$

You may have more or fewer rows; this is just an example. Remember that this is your (or your and your partner's) scorecard, not anyone else's! It does not matter how you compare to others. It doesn't matter if the total is negative! What's important is that you start tracking. You need to be honest with the values. Asset values should reflect the market value if you sold it that day. Cars should be the Kelly Blue Book value, and houses can be Zillow or Redfin estimates.

I've seen some people include "other assets" like clothes. If it is your intent to sell these items, you regularly do so, and you have itemized values, then I guess it's okay. Otherwise, no. You may have just purchased some nice furniture. That's great! But it is not an asset; it was an expense. You're not going to resell that sofa. Remember, the point is to be honest with yourself, not artificially inflate your values. Personally, I would not track these extraneous items, and they will show up on this sheet as cash in Checking or Savings if they are actually sold.

Alright, I did it. Why is this so important?

Your first data point is complete, excellent! As months and years go by and you add more data points, you're going to start seeing some trends. You will have visual evidence of your financial behavior. One big lesson should have already emerged. Net worth has two levers: assets and liabilities. You should see that you have two options to increase your net worth:

1) Increasing your assets, or

2) Decreasing your liabilities.

We're going to do both.

CHAPTER 3
CRAFT A SAFETY NET

The Most Important Financial Instrument: Cash

It's time to have a conversation about the most important financial instrument that exists. Roth IRA? No. 401(k)? No. Index funds? No. I am talking about cash. Cash doesn't just refer to paper money; it includes all money that can be quickly accessed. For our purposes, the money in checking, savings, and money market accounts is going to be referred to as cash.

The purpose of cash isn't to grow your net worth, but to avoid disaster. In the initial stage, having a sufficient amount of cash will shield you from being forced to take on crippling debt, should the unexpected occur. I used to wonder: if I were let go tomorrow, what would I have to show in the bank for all of my work, and how would I live until I found my next job?

The most important part of personal finance is having enough cash to cover your living expenses. Cash is the lifeblood of a business, and it's no different for personal finance. It doesn't matter how much money you have if you can't access it. The initial goal here is one month of living expenses in checking, two months of living expenses in savings. If you've made it to this point, congrats! This is a huge milestone. If not, that's okay! Please keep reading. The following chapters should provide some help.

There are more benefits to cash that we'll discuss later, but what's amazing is that this doesn't even have to be thought of as dead money. High-yield savings accounts

(HYSA) pay a solid interest rate, and some companies offer investor checking accounts that pay similar rates, far higher than traditional bank accounts. It can be a pain to switch to a new account, but it's a one-time hassle and will result in years of higher returns.

Insurance

Again, this chapter is about crafting your safety net. At the least, you need high-deductible insurance to protect your health, your house, and your car. This is about avoiding disaster. If you have dependents, you should have some life insurance, which may be included in your job benefits.

CHAPTER 4
LET'S TALK ABOUT INTEREST RATES, RATES OF RETURN, AND CREDIT CARDS

Frankly, let's not. I'm going to be honest, I really don't want to talk about interest rates and rates of return. I can hear the air going out of the balloon just reading that chapter title. It just sounds so boring. Alright, I'll make it quick. 4%, 10%, 20%. These numbers will vary by a percent or two and will be impacted by a litany of factors, but don't get hung up on that here; that's not the point. Here's what these numbers represent:

4%: The interest rate you earn from a HYSA

10%: The historical annualized rate of return of the S&P 500 stock index

20%: The interest rate you pay on credit card debt

20% is just absurd. It is double the amount that we're planning to return on our long-term stock holdings. It is so absurd that if someone is promising an annual 20% return, it is probably fraudulent. You cannot expect to earn 20% on your money every year. Credit card debt is the equivalent of a hole in the bottom of your financial ship. Fix it now! We must have zero credit card debt going forward.

That doesn't mean to not use credit cards, but the full statement balance must be paid every month. Remember from the net worth exercise that our goal is to grow our assets and decrease our liabilities. How can we expect to reach financial freedom if we're receiving 4% and 10% rates of return on our money, yet paying 20%? We can't. Credit card debt is toxic. It has to be eliminated.

You can start to tackle this by paying down either the highest interest rate loan or the lowest balance. I'd recommend starting with the lowest balance for a few reasons:

1) It will be less intimidating and you'll have more confidence that you can do it.

2) It will feel so freaking good once you pay off a debt and you'll ride that positive feeling to pay off other balances.

3) Having fewer debt accounts will reduce complexity.

4) The difference in interest rates between the accounts is not as important as the behavior and mindset that comes from getting rid of these debts.

If you've paid off your credit card debt in full, congratulations!! You've achieved one of the most important financial milestones of your life. The amount of interest that you won't be paying for the rest of your life is unbelievably immense, and your behavior and mindset will carry you throughout the rest of your life, pre- and post-retirement. Still working on it? No worries! The following chapters should provide more help.

CHAPTER 5 THROW "NORMAL" IN THE GARBAGE

If you haven't already, please let go of trying to be "normal." Financial freedom is not normal. Early retirement is definitely not normal. This is a rare path, mainly because it's not built on selling you something. We live in a consumption culture. Most people spend whatever they earn. Companies are extremely good at marketing and selling you things that you don't need. Social media shows the highlight reel of people's lives. The financial industry wants you to keep working because their fees are structured so that they get a percentage off of the money you've accrued. The longer you work, the more money they make.

For most people, the deck is stacked against them. They look at others to try to define what is normal. New cars? Normal. Newest cell phone? Normal. Expensive vacations? Normal. Credit card debt? Sadly, normal. Social media has made it that much harder. It's no longer just about seeing how your neighbors and coworkers behave; social media is playing the highlight reels 24/7 online from people with whom you don't even interact.

The way to combat this is to first recognize what you're up against. Advertisements are everywhere, in many forms, and are extremely effective. Companies pay millions of dollars to try to convince you that buying their product is normal. That's all it is. In fact, they've gotten so good at it that people are advertising their products for them for free by wearing their logos. Giant check marks on shoes. Genius!

I'll give credit where credit is due. Frankly, it's pretty impressive how they've done it. I'm not saying that I'm immune to this either; it's just important to recognize how the system works.

In general, I don't fault people for the way they behave. Most people's behavior is shaped as a response to their environment and what they believe are societal norms. I don't think that most people spend with proper intentionality. If they do, their spending habits are likely driven by other people.

We are not going to base our spending or finances on other people. We have a clear goal of financial freedom, and that is going to strongly influence our spending. Our spending is going to be 100% driven by our needs and our family's needs. We are not going to be influenced or care how others spend their money. Not that it matters, but we have no idea what their finances look like. Similarly, we're not going to care what others might think about how we spend our money. We're playing a different game than everyone else. As such, don't look for external validation; it's going to have to be internal.

CHAPTER 6
EXPENSES ARE INFINITELY MORE IMPORTANT THAN INCOME

Expenses are the most important factor in personal finance. It doesn't matter if someone has a high income if they also have high expenses. Expenses create the margin needed to build your net worth machine. Expenses represent the baseline to determine when you have enough money and can retire. Income isn't even part of the equation. Expenses are that important!

You don't have control over rates of return. You have limited control over your income. The good news is that you do have control over your expenses. You have the ability to set your own formula for when you will have enough money to retire. Incredible!

The math will always say to flatly reduce, but I don't necessarily believe that. All else equal, you will reach financial freedom faster by reducing expenses, but saying to reduce everything is simple, bad advice. This is your life. I'm not going to tell you what is important to you. Our goal is to reduce our baseline living expenses, where able, and maximize our "fun fund." I am all for spending money on things that you find fun. These activities create lasting memories that you will have for the rest of your life. If something doesn't fall into this category, then it's a necessary, baseline living expense. If it doesn't fit within that narrow description, then it's likely waste that can be eliminated.

We are going to be intentional with every purchase that we make. Every dollar serves a purpose. If it doesn't generate fun or fit the definition of a necessary, baseline living expense, then we can put it to work in our net worth machine. By having control over our expenses, not only are we reducing the number that we need to reach for financial freedom, but we are also increasing our liquid assets, allowing us to reach that number even faster.

This is not about deprivation. Some might call it deferred gratification, but I don't think that's accurate either. I enjoy saving money. That saved money has a purpose. It can easily be quantified. By not buying something I don't need, I just saved $x (plus 10% every year). By looking at the weekly grocery circular, I can buy the same thing this week for half of what it will cost next week. I get that satisfaction immediately. It's not deferred gratification; it's different gratification. Taking control of your life and working towards a financial goal is gratifying, not just in the future, but in the moment. Some tips on expenses:

Cars

Unless you live in a city with excellent public transportation, you're probably going to need a car. The goal is to find a quality, reliable car that will last for a long time. Cars have a very specific purpose, and that is to get you from point A to point B. That's it. If your vehicle is for work, then you may need slightly more functionality. If you spend a lot of time in your car, then I can understand a certain level of physical comfort. Anything more than needed functionality is waste.

There is no need to routinely drive different cars, and a monthly car payment is not a requirement. My wife and I have had the same cars for fifteen years, and I can't imagine how much money we've saved by driving these vehicles. The least expensive car is likely the one that you are currently driving. If always driving a new car means a lot to you (and is not based on what you think others might think of you), then you need to recognize that the true cost is many years of freedom and retirement.

Housing

Entire books have been written on this topic. Here's my advice: just don't over-extend yourself. You don't have to buy property. Buying a house is a big deal. Transaction costs are very high in real estate, and moving is notoriously awful. I view buying a house as long-term, at least ten years, but ideally as long as possible. Housing prices don't always go up. Even if they do, they've likely gone up everywhere, so you haven't really gained anything. Even if you are mortgage-free, housing costs will never be zero. You will still have high costs for property taxes, home insurance, repairs, and maintenance. Whether you rent or buy, housing is always a huge expense.

Well, that sounds awful. Why would I ever buy a house? It is about a sense of control and permanence. Moving sucks. You don't want to have to move because your landlord wants to sell the property. Also, banks are not landlords. You have 100% equity in your house. As long as you pay your debt in accordance with the mortgage contract, there's nothing that the bank can do. Homes are tracked as assets in your net worth with the corresponding mortgage as a liability. When you buy a house, your net worth doesn't change. Assets and liabilities both go up, while the down payment shifts from cash into implied home equity (home value minus mortgage amount). The purpose of home ownership is not about making money. Any gains with home ownership are just paper gains. As the saying goes, you cannot eat your home equity.

I don't see this written enough, but make sure that you are getting "bang for your buck" out of your property taxes. It doesn't matter whether you explicitly pay them as a homeowner or they are baked into your rent; look at what these property taxes provide. Public schools, parks, libraries, walking/biking trails, community events, etc. These are all services that you have already paid for with your property taxes. They're now free for you to use. Use them and connect with others in your community!

Food

You should cook as many meals as you can at home. It's cheaper and healthier than eating out. In the case where it isn't cheaper, then it is certainly much healthier. Restaurant delivery companies are the worst offenders in this sphere. Combining restaurants with food delivery costs seems extremely excessive and can easily be eliminated.

Look at your grocery store's weekly circular. It only takes a few minutes. I often pick my weekly meals based on what is on sale. You'll also learn the patterns for when your staples go on sale and can stock up during those weeks. The same items can vary wildly in price from week to week.

Warehouse stores can provide some value, as long as you use them. Buying non-perishable items in bulk is a no-brainer. Produce and other perishables may spoil too quickly, so it may be best to avoid them.

Contracted Work

I've heard the saying that if contracted work costs less than your hourly wage, then you should pay someone else to do it. Wait, what?! Does this make any sense? Be honest with yourself. If you have the ability to earn an hourly wage at any time of the day and you're forgoing that hourly wage to do the task, then I can see the argument, but that seems rare. Even rarer when you factor in that the fully loaded hourly price of the contracted work, which is generally expensive, must be lower than your hourly wage for the argument to have validity.

You should run everything through a filter of "Can I do this myself?" If not, why not? House cleaning is an easy one. Landscaping is labor-intensive, but you get to immediately see and appreciate the work that you just completed. Appliance repair is often pretty easy, and the diagnoses are generally widely available online. Same for electrical and plumbing.

I'm not suggesting that you do everything yourself, but you need to first run it through that filter. There are many benefits to do-it-yourself projects:

1) It costs less,

2) you learn new skills,

3) you get the satisfaction of completing the job yourself and give yourself confidence that you can try other new things,

4) you get cool new tools,

5) you'll likely be humbled and will gain an appreciation for people that do this for a living, and

6) if it turns out that you can't fix it, it's okay! After all, you can always hire a professional.

Entertainment

I'm a huge proponent of fun and entertainment. The problem is that some costs often shift from one-time fun experiences to baseline living expenses that don't bring the same enjoyment. Carefully review subscriptions and recurring experiences and think about what you're getting out of these costs. Always look for new ways to have fun. Also, fun doesn't have to be expensive.

Home Furnishings

Pay for quality, beware of cheap. The goal is to buy something that will last for decades. If you're considering replacing something simply for aesthetic purposes, deeply question why you're doing it and the lasting satisfaction that it will bring you. Changing for function and utility is fine. If your motivation is based on what others might think or what HGTV tells you is "normal," deeply question it.

Final Thoughts on Expenses

Expenses are going to fluctuate as you go through different phases of life. Still, the key is to spend with intentionality. Your motivation should be internal to live a life consistent with your values. Think of saving money as buying time. Small expenses can add up, but big, frivolous expenses are undoubtedly adding years to your working life.

This is about developing a behavior and a mindset. It is about discipline and gaining more control over your life. By doing this, you will find that you will create sustainable habits that you don't even think about. The increased self-control will bring about self-confidence and will translate into other fields.

Above all, enjoy the journey. Saving money can be fun and addictive, but it isn't the only thing; live your life. Experience fun, culture, and the arts. These are what make you feel the bounds of human emotion, push your brain out of routine, and provide an invaluable perspective that cannot be quantified. We'll spend what we have to spend on expenses, but remember to save room for fun.

CHAPTER 7
LET'S BUILD, BABY

Alright, enough is enough, let's start to build this machine. We aren't going to aim for a certain savings percentage. We are going to throw every dollar we can at this. No, do not take on debt just to buy assets. That is dangerous and, frankly, unnecessary. Charlie Munger's famous saying is "Invert, always invert." The idea is to go beyond thinking about what it takes to achieve a goal and instead, think about what it would take to destroy that goal, and make sure that you avoid that activity. A lender calling in a short-term debt that you are leveraging to purchase long-term assets qualifies as a disaster. This is the same mindset behind why crafting a safety net and controlling expenses are so important.

There are so many investment options, how do I start?

There certainly are, and it can be daunting trying to figure out what everything means. Financial professionals love it because this complexity creates an industry for them to service. Intimidated? Not to worry! Anyone can learn the basics. It's not that hard. Don't think that you ever need to know everything in this sphere. Investing doesn't have to be complex. There are only a few things that you're going to need to know.

Please understand that I am not a CPA or CFP. The financial instruments discussed below are US-focused. Keep in mind that the IRS may make tweaks to the rules of these accounts each year. Check the IRS website (irs.gov) for the full definition, specifics, and current contribution limits for these accounts.

Roth Accounts (After-Tax)

Roth accounts include money that has already been taxed, but is able to grow and be withdrawn tax-free. This is the king of retirement account types. In retirement and later in life, you'll find that you are trying to maximize ways to move money from the other account types into Roth accounts. More on that later.

There is one significant, additional key benefit to Roth accounts: Roth contributions (not gains) can be withdrawn at any time, without penalty. This is the money that was taxed when it entered the account. We never want to have to withdraw these funds early; that's why we have cash, but it is nice to know that we have this option in the event of an actual emergency. Any other funds withdrawn before age 59.5 are subject to taxes and penalties.

Traditional Retirement Accounts (Deferred Tax)

The key benefit of these accounts is that the contributions and gains are not taxed until they are withdrawn in retirement. Putting money into these accounts can lower your current taxable income, which may specifically benefit high earners. Funds withdrawn before age 59.5 are subject to taxes and penalties.

Brokerage Accounts (Taxable)

These are not generally considered "retirement accounts" because funds can be withdrawn at any time, without penalty, and they don't include the special tax provisions of Roth or traditional retirement accounts. You will have to open this account on your own outside of your employer through a brokerage firm (Charles Schwab, Fidelity, Vanguard, etc). This account has been labeled a "leaky bucket" because, unlike retirement accounts, you will pay taxes every year on this account for interest, dividends, and any realized capital gains. While the other two accounts are generally built for a traditional retirement, this is the account that will fuel our early retirement.

So Which Account Should I Choose?

From a simple math perspective, the determination of whether to fund a Roth or traditional account comes down to whether you believe that your income taxes will be higher today or when the money is withdrawn in retirement. Are taxes lower today? Roth. Are taxes higher today? Traditional. Incomes generally increase over a career, which means that you'll likely want to fund Roth accounts early in your working career, then gradually shift to traditional accounts in your highest earning years, when your income taxes are nearing their peak. In reality, you're going to want both of these accounts.

An amazing thing about retirement is that you will be able to determine your own taxable income, to a degree. There's no way to get around taxes for interest and dividends in your brokerage account. Still, after that, you will be able to control whether you use cash, sell stocks in your brokerage account (long-term capital gains tax), withdraw from a traditional retirement account (all taxable), or withdraw from a Roth account (not taxable). Account diversity gives you options, flexibility, and control.

Ok, I'm Getting There – Is There a Specific Order to Funding These Accounts?

Before we start funding our early retirement, we need to make sure that our traditional retirement period is funded. Defined pensions are nearly dead in this country, so employers are offering Roth 401(k) and traditional 401(k) retirement accounts. The 401(k) nomenclature refers to the IRS code for this type of employer-sponsored retirement account. Depending on your employer, you may instead have a TSP or 403(b). It's a different IRS code, but these accounts function the same way with the same contribution limits.

As a benefit, many employers will match your retirement contribution, up to a specific amount. Make sure that you get this match! It is free money. The amount that the IRS allows you to contribute to these accounts varies, normally with slight increases each year. Fund as much as you can up to the maximum amount. There are no income limits to this type of Roth account. With all of these accounts, make sure to actually purchase funds once money is in the account. My recommendation is 85% US large-cap funds, 15% international funds. Entire books have been written regarding portfolio allocation. That's not this book. This allocation provides a good enough approach to capture the winners of the broad market.

I Did It! I've Maxed Out my Retirement Accounts. What's Next?

Oh, heck yeah, you are crushing it! It's time to start building our early retirement fund. You've already automated your retirement contributions. Whatever is left after your expenses and above your cash safety net is going to go into your brokerage account. What should we buy with this money? Index funds. All index funds.

Index funds are a non-actively managed portfolio of funds that are meant to replicate an index. So, what is so great about index funds?

1) Diversity; we are investing in the market as a whole, not one individual company.

2) Simplicity; we don't need hundreds of individual stock holdings.

3) Low fees; these are not actively managed funds, so the fees for the fund manager to maintain these funds are very low.

4) Ease; we have a system, and we don't have to analyze individual companies every time we are ready to buy.

Again, my recommendation here is 85% in an S&P 500 index fund, 15% in an international fund. There are no contribution limits to brokerage accounts, so you can contribute as much as you like. These are great for flexibility, and you do get lower federal tax rates for long-term capital gains and qualified dividends.

There are ways to access money in retirement accounts prior to age 59.5, but that's not going to be how we base our plan. We want to keep that money in those accounts, compounding year over year, for as long as possible.

I Have Children, Should I Fund a 529?

Yes, if you can. Contributions to these accounts have been taxed, but they grow tax-free. They can be withdrawn tax-free for qualified education expenses. In addition, some states offer a tax deduction, up to a specified amount, for 529 contributions in a year. Flexibility has recently been added to the tax code, which allows for some of these funds to go towards Roth IRA contributions for the beneficiary in the future.

I've Heard Some Amazing Things About Health Savings Accounts (HSAs)

If you are healthy and don't have a lot of medical expenses, then yes, you should consider a high-deductible health plan with an HSA. It is likely the least expensive option, and it allows you to make voluntary pre-tax contributions, up to a specified contribution limit. These have extremely strong tax benefits: tax-free contributions, tax-free growth, and tax-free withdrawals for qualified expenses. It's possible to even withdraw from this account for non-medical expenses without penalty at age 65 and beyond, with the withdrawals taxed in the same manner as a traditional retirement account. You should run the numbers on your health plan options and medical expenses. Still, it is hard to argue against the advantages of HSA accounts.

What About Real Estate? I've Heard that Rental Property Can Be Lucrative

First of all, it's not necessary. You can invest your money in the stock market and be fine. Secondly, it depends on how involved you want to be. It's not completely passive income. You have to think of it like running a business. Things break. Tenants might not pay. Your tenant might not renew their lease, and you'll have to find a new tenant. The property may not appreciate the way you hoped. You may get stuck with a big tax bill for capital gains and depreciation recapture if you decide to sell.

If you run the numbers and know what you're getting into, it can be a good way to earn a monthly income. Just know that it will require more effort, will be harder to liquidate, will add tax complexity, may require more stress than other ways of investing, and may come with a lower return on investment.

CHAPTER 8
MY MACHINE IS GROWING, MY EXPENSES ARE IN CHECK, WHAT ELSE CAN I DO?

Whew. Alright. Our foundation is set. That was a lot. Now it's time to focus on how to best optimize our machine to keep this thing growing. Back to the net worth statement!

Monitoring Net Worth

This is going to be our scorecard throughout to show how we're progressing. As such, you're probably going to want to update it frequently. I get it. You're excited. You want tangible evidence to see how you're doing. I was the same way. Currently, I update mine every six months. However, when I first started, I was updating it with every paycheck. This is dangerous behavior. Why? It's very short-sighted, and you'll think that your finances are at the whims of daily market fluctuations. If you check frequently, you are guaranteeing that you will see it go down. You'll then question whether this is the right strategy. This is the point where most people fail. The only thing that can derail your progress on this financial journey is changing your strategy. Remember, invert, always invert. What can derail you on your path to financial freedom? You, if you change your strategy.

In reality, we don't care about daily market movements. We will be in this thing for decades. Decades. This may be a good time to think more deeply about the S&P 500 index funds. What exactly are we buying? We are buying the biggest and strongest companies that are using every inch of advantage that they have to maximize profits.

Additionally, it self-regulates. Companies that lose their competitive advantages are dropped; rising powers are automatically added. We don't have to do any of this balancing ourselves. That hot, incredible company that everyone is talking about?

We likely already own it. The companies in this index are working around the clock to innovate, find new efficiencies, and use their market power. Do we have the market advantages of these companies?

Of course not. The good news?

We don't have to. We can buy these companies through S&P 500 index funds and receive a payoff from all of their hard work and market advantages.

You're Going to Have to Resist Your Own Urges

You're becoming more financially savvy, you're building a bankroll, and as such, you might start to think that you have an edge. Why? Because you're smart. I won't argue that at all. You are definitely smart. Who in the world would still be reading to this point? You are rare.

The problem is that smart does not equal success in investing. The finance industry is a minefield for people who are just smart enough to get involved. Options, individual stocks, commodities, crypto, forex, "stock market is expensive," "buy the dip," etc. So many ways to try to show how smart you are. It's a massive industry that tries to exploit our egos to get us to try to beat the market. There's not much that you can control in this life, but you can control yourself.

We aren't trying to beat the market. We aren't gambling on financial instruments and timing markets. We aren't traders; we are long-term investors. Our strategy is to buy the best companies that use their advantages to make profits. We'll gladly take our 10% average annual returns. There is a proven system to get you to your goal. You don't have to be novel in your approach.

You'll hear that investing is about "buying low and selling high." It's not. That's still trading. We are going to buy whenever we can and hold for as long as possible. Decades. Investing is about being disciplined and consistent. It's not about showing how smart we are. It's about overcoming our urges. Be especially careful during political transitions.

Half of the country is afraid that the elected party will destroy everything, while the other half is convinced that stocks will go to the moon. The media loves to play on this explosive polarity because the country is behaving wildly emotionally, and they can use it to generate clicks. Stand pat and play the long game. Can you imagine if 24/7 cable networks gave this advice every day? That would be so boring, and no one would watch. Ohhh, I get it. That's not financial advice. That's entertainment.

Still want to engage in trading? Just acknowledge that it's gambling. It's entertainment. Think deeply about what you are getting from this activity and whether it's necessary, because it's not about making money. It's an expense.

Analyzing Net Worth Trends

Ok, back to the net worth statement. You should start to see a few trends emerging.

1) By reducing your liabilities, you have directly increased your net worth. It shows up as a 1:1 impact on the statement, but in reality, paying off a liability is worth much more when you factor in all of the interest that you no longer have to pay. Keep getting rid of these debts, although I'm not talking about your mortgage; more on that later. How could we not address that age-old question?

2) Car values are decreasing. It's not fun to see an asset value decrease, but it shows how vehicles are a drag on your net worth.

3) Your net worth isn't growing as fast as you'd hoped.

You're going to find that although your machine is doing some work through asset appreciation and reduced drag from liabilities, the vast majority of the changes are coming directly from your contributions. This is tough. Really tough. It is very hard to grow the machine when it is all up to your individual savings. It's almost unfair to think that the hardest part of saving and growing your money is when you are just starting out and have the least. It's easy to see why the deck is stacked against you and why so many people fail.

Let's Talk About Income, Finally

Alright, you've backed me into a corner. I can't get around it any longer. Outside of expenses, the amount that you can save and add to your machine is a direct result of your income. We've talked about expenses. We can now, finally, talk about income.

Although I'm a firm believer that a broad education and breadth of experiences help you become a more well-rounded person, when it comes to a career and making money, the focus should be on depth. When you enter a career field, your goal should be to become a technical expert. Find your niche and ride it. Strive to be someone that companies need. Eventually, your knowledge and experience will make you invaluable. If you're early in your career, you won't have knowledge or experience. All you have is your labor. Employers want hard workers with good attitudes. Set yourself apart by your work ethic and attitude.

I don't believe that "hustling" outside of your career field will be nearly as lucrative as acquiring depth within it. Use this extra energy to make yourself more valuable to your company. Training classes? You bet. Professional certification that your company endorses? Absolutely. Graduate degree? Definitely a possibility. If it will make you more valuable and increase your skills, it's a no-brainer. Look for opportunities and seize them when they appear. You don't want to miss out on the perfect opportunity because you aren't prepared.

Transitioning to Management

You'll likely come to a point in your career where you will hit your ceiling as an employee, and the only way to advance is by taking on a completely different job: manager. I don't know if anyone is ever truly prepared for this switch. You'll still be regarded as a technical expert. Still, this job is about completely different skills: resource management, human engagement, and communication. The good news is that these are all skills that can be improved. Imposter syndrome and unease from always being "the adult in the room" are common, but you'll get used to it.

Working in management allows you to share your knowledge with others and help them in their personal growth. The hardest part of being a manager is that you're in charge of far more work than you can do yourself. Excelling in management means asking for help. Help from your employees, employer, and peers. Management is hard. You are always under-resourced. The job requires you to focus on efficiency. With that said, don't avoid management. It's not that bad. It will force you to develop new skills. You can do it.

Additional Income Tips

It's time to liquidate some of those "other assets." I know I gave you a hard time in Chapter 2 about mislabeling these things as assets. If we want them to be assets, we need to turn them into cash. Have any video games, movies, books, or anything else in your house that you don't use anymore? Online marketplaces are great ways to sell these items. I still don't think anyone is going to buy that old sofa, but now is your time to prove me wrong.

The First $100,000

Raising a newborn baby is hard, thankless work. Bear with me here. Sleepless nights. Constant effort. Overbearing responsibility. Emotions drained. The worst part is that the baby doesn't even smile for the first few months. It's a constant fight. You're doing everything you can, but you're not seeing the results that you want. There's no appreciation. But then, out of nowhere, you look down, and your baby is smiling. There it is. Joy. Congratulations on your first $100k.

CHAPTER 9
THIS IS GREAT. HOW WILL I KNOW WHEN I HAVE ENOUGH TO RETIRE?

Great question! I'm also glad that you used the term enough. Much of our culture is based on the belief that you can never have enough. This is completely false! This chapter will show you how to determine the exact number that you need.

Your Financial Freedom Number

The formula for finding your financial freedom number is shockingly simple. Annual Expenses x 25. That's it. That's the "back of a napkin" math. Have a great day, that's it for me.

Woah, Woah, Woah, That's Far Too Simplistic

You're right, it is. There are qualifiers, so let's get into the components.

1) The number has to be in liquid assets. For our purposes, that includes cash, retirement, and brokerage accounts. You have to be able to withdraw the money. As such, home equity does not factor into your number. Home equity is part of your net worth, I won't argue that, but it does not matter at all in this equation. Rental property isn't included here either, but you can reduce your needed withdrawals by the net cash flow of the business. From this point on, we're going to include a new line in our net worth statement for our total liquid assets. Total net worth

doesn't really matter anymore. Total liquid assets are the number that we care about.

2) This is based on the "4% rule," developed by Bill Bengen in 1994. He demonstrated that an initial withdrawal amount of 4% (then subsequently increased annually for inflation) on a portfolio (50/50 stocks and bonds) would have never gone to zero over any historical 30-year period. Thus, 4% became known as the safe withdrawal rate (SWR). Since portfolio withdrawals are based on expenses, this is how the 25x expenses equation is derived.

This rule is inherently conservative. It represents the absolute worst-case scenario over any 30 years in US history. Since 1994, he has updated his research to show that the SWR is 4.7% with broader asset allocation. In fact, he says the average SWR over the last 100 years is actually 7%. He personally recommends using 5.25 to 5.5%.

Additionally, it assumes that your expenses will increase every year due to inflation. This doesn't have to be the case. We've shown control over our expenses. It is possible to forego a vacation if absolutely necessary. It also assumes that you will never receive additional income. It's okay to plan that way, but it may not represent reality. We haven't accounted at all for Social Security, which is future income. Additionally, if you currently have a mortgage, it will eventually be paid off in the future if you don't move, which will reduce expenses.

3) You need to account for taxes. You will need to look at how much money you need to withdraw from your accounts (and which specific account) and take the

tax burden into the equation. Realized capital gains, dividends, and interest all carry a tax burden. Luckily, you will still be able to use the standard or itemized tax deductions. We want to start withdrawals from our brokerage account. Still, it's important to know that there are ways to access the money in your retirement account prior to age 59.5 without penalty, if needed. A substantially equal periodic payment (SEPP) plan allows for withdrawals, but has limited flexibility once begun.

A Roth conversion ladder strategy is another method. Funds can be converted from traditional retirement accounts to Roth accounts, with the conversion amount allowed to be withdrawn from the Roth account after a five-year waiting period without penalty. The idea is to do a Roth conversion every year for the amount that you will need to spend in five years in the future. Then, at that future date, you can withdraw the converted funds from the Roth account without additional taxes or penalty. Keep in mind that you will have to pay taxes for the conversion in the year that the conversion is performed. Long story short, \$100 worth of living expenses may require more than \$100 worth of withdrawals from your liquid accounts.

4) You need to know your annual expenses. Yes, the importance of expenses should now be glaringly obvious. You may think that you have a good estimate of what you spend. Still, I recommend computing your actual yearly expenses on an annual basis at least five years before you retire. This is an unbiased, backward-looking process that can easily

be done by looking at annual credit card statements and banking withdrawals.

I am okay with separating something that is truly a "one-time" expense. Still, after a few years, you'll likely find that you always have a few "one-time" expenses, so just include them in your number. This process will compute your actual expenses, but it should also give you confidence that you will know and be able to confidently project what your lifestyle will cost in the future. Use your actual expenses as your baseline and add what you believe will be additional costs in retirement, notably, health care.

Health care is likely the biggest boogeyman that keeps people working longer than they need. However, like any other expense, the cost of health insurance can be quantified and added to your projected annual expenses. Go to healthcare.gov, choose your state, enter your planned retirement income (not current income), and look at the options and prices. Add this number to your annual expenses, and voila, we've now accounted for health insurance.

Some Things to Think About

You likely don't need to add any additional buffer to this number, since this is already based on the worst-case scenario for market returns. In addition to the conservatism built into the 4% rule, your expenses in retirement will likely go down. Work and commute expenses disappear. You will be able to eat more meals at home. Without work stress, you may not have a need for expensive stress-relieving habits and experiences. You will also have more flexibility when you can travel, which can greatly reduce travel costs.

What is the Lifestyle that You Want?

I hope you've been thinking about this. It's time to put some reality into what your retirement lifestyle will cost. Using actual expenses may be sufficient, but if there are other big expenses that you would like in retirement, they need to be added to your number. Travel is absolutely a worthwhile endeavor, but beware the upsell spending traps in the industry. You should be able to quantify first-class or private travel and see its impact on your numbers. Think hard about what you are getting for it. If that is the lifestyle that you want, that's okay, but it will force you to work longer.

The "Eighth Wonder of the World," Compound Interest

This is going to take a while. It is not a "get-rich-quick" scheme. This is about developing a behavior and being consistent and disciplined. You'll find that the growth is going to be based on what Albert Einstein has named the "Eighth Wonder of the World," compound interest. "He who understands it, earns it. He who doesn't, pays it." The formula is simple, but powerful. Amount = principal x (1 + annual rate) ^time.

We won't address the annual rate, because we are sticking with our 10% average annual return index funds. The most exciting part of this equation is that it is exponential. This is incredible, and what makes this formula so powerful. Most people think linearly, but I've noticed that most things in this world actually function exponentially. When you monitor your net worth changes, the line of best fit will most closely resemble a linear equation for many years. This is because the addition to the principal through your savings is doing most of the heavy lifting. However, after a while, time takes over. The issue, inherently, is that it takes time for this formula to become powerful. If you stay consistent, time will make this formula explosive, and the gains will far exceed the income from your job, which will be hard to comprehend.

Additional Tips

At some point, it will sink in how simply this process works. Life is complex; money isn't. Once you know the system, it comes down to consistency. You want to take your own possible errors out of the equation. In investing, your best move is generally to do nothing when others are panicking. Your biggest mistakes will come from trying to time the market. Automation is your friend. Automation is forced consistency. Strive for simple over complex. Complexity will find you; don't seek it out. Patience over cleverness. The key is patience and discipline.

Choose your partner wisely. This is good advice, in general, but it specifically applies to finance as well. Money is often cited as a topic of consternation among couples. Make sure that you and your partner are on the same page about values and plans for this journey. My wife and I are extremely similar in our spending habits, which was crucial for this process. I couldn't have retired on this timeline alone. If you have children, make wills for yourself and your spouse and register them with the county. It's easy to find a sample for your state online for free. You can have them notarized with witnesses to avoid probate. Even if you only have one child, it's important to designate legal guardianship if anything happens to you and your spouse.

At some point, you'll find that you will have more than enough money in your retirement accounts for a traditional retirement. You can compute this by using the compound interest formula to see what your retirement balance is projected to grow to when you can withdraw penalty-free at age 59.5. This is a major milestone! At this point, I recommend reducing your retirement contributions to the minimum required for a match from your employer and instead putting all of your new contributions into your brokerage account. It's not as tax-efficient, but it is much more flexible. This is your early retirement account.

The Concept of "Sequence of Returns Risk"

Although the S&P 500 has returned an average of about 10% annually since its inception in 1957, the actual annual returns have varied wildly from 25% in 2024 to an 18% loss in 2018. The concept of sequence of returns means that even if the average annual return is 10%, the total portfolio can vary wildly depending on when market drops occur, notably at the beginning of retirement. Basically, people have a fear that the market will drop for the first few years immediately after they retire, and they'll never be able to rebuild a large enough portfolio for a viable retirement. The hypothetical higher returns later in retirement won't be enough to offset the hypothetical losses early in retirement.

A few things here. First, the 4% rule already accounts for actual returns. The sequence of returns concept is a hypothetical exercise. It is a mildly interesting look at how math works, but nothing more. No one has a crystal ball for future annual returns, but at least the 4% rule is based on historical returns. Second, there is a way to offset this risk. You guessed it, cash. I recommend having three years of living expenses in cash in retirement so that if there is a significant market event, you aren't forced to sell stock. It's not about buying low and selling high; it is about not selling low. Cash is your buffer. If nothing else, cash is your peace of mind for sequence of returns risk.

"The Waiting is the Hardest Part"

There will come a point where your machine will be humming, and you will be so good at regulating your expenses that it will just depend on time. This can be a very hard period because you don't have control to make it go any faster. Absolutely do not stop having fun! You're at the point where spending a little more money is not going to make much of a difference at this point anyways.

You're likely going to be laser-focused on your number, but there's very little that you can do to get there faster. My advice: develop and get lost in your hobbies. It's easy to say that hobbies aren't important, but they are. They are incredibly important. They are an outlet for your creativity and brainpower that is completely disassociated from making money. It's a huge leg up for your transition to retirement.

Spend time with your friends and family. Try out new things. Anything that will distract you from staring at the clock. Go outside and experience nature. Stay humble. Keep in mind that most people are struggling. You're going to want to help others with financial knowledge, but it can be complicated. Start with the basics and retirement accounts. I don't see a reason to ever disclose personal net worth numbers with anyone. The key to financial freedom is withdrawal rate; that's the goal.

Bonus Topic: Should I Pay Off the Mortgage?

There's no way I was going to be able to get through this without addressing everyone's favorite personal finance question: paying off the mortgage. If you pay off the mortgage early, your expenses will go down because you no longer have to make monthly principal and interest payments. Keep in mind that your housing expenses won't drop to zero; you will still have to pay property taxes and insurance, which are significant expenses. If you itemize your taxes and deduct mortgage interest, then that should be part of the math as well. Be cognizant that selling stocks to pay off the mortgage will trigger capital gains. Always maintain a large enough cash balance.

In general, I view paying off a mortgage as a luxury, not a necessity. It shouldn't be considered until after all of your other financial milestones have been accomplished. I would much rather have the flexibility of a significant liquid amount than a paid-off house. If you were one of the lucky ones to lock in a low fixed rate during COVID-19, it would be extremely hard to justify ever paying that off early.

CHAPTER 10
THIS IS CRAZY, I MAY ACTUALLY BE ABLE TO RETIRE EARLY. I'M SO EXCITED. I'M SO EXCITED. I'M SO SCARED.

Incredible, we actually made it. Financial freedom is here. It's going to be surreal, and it won't make sense. What you may not imagine is how quickly the feeling shifts from joy to anxiety. The goal that you have been pursuing for many years is now gone. The thought of forgoing future income and living solely off your assets is scary. What will I do with my time? How will others react? It's going to be hard to translate how numbers on a spreadsheet can permit a major life event. That's what retirement is. It is a major life event. It is a big, big deal. It will rewire your brain. It will force you to see the world in a completely different way. It's so impactful that I felt compelled to dedicate the entire second half of this book to talking about it.

Trust the Math

Don't change what got you here. There's no reason to add complexity. We already discussed the components of the 4% rule and the sequence of returns risk. If you feel compelled to add more buffer, keep adding to your cash balance. There is always a boogeyman. Fear is a survival instinct that is ingrained in our DNA. We can't get rid of it. Fear can be useful when it makes us think about worst-case scenarios and how we can adapt. It's detrimental when it causes paralysis and isn't based on reality. There are always articles about how the stock market is "about to crash." I find that a remedy for anxiety is information. In this realm, we can quantify the boogeyman. If there is a scenario that concerns you, run the numbers and see the impact. A major concern that keeps people working longer is health care, but it can be quantified. Go to healthcare.gov and actually run the numbers. Also, you may be shocked by how much healthier your life can be in retirement.

What is the Lifestyle that You Want?

After you reach "enough," you'll get to a point when you question why you're trading your time and energy for money that you don't need. The time has come. You need to be able to clearly answer why you want to retire. It may have been a pipe dream earlier, but now it's a reality. If you can't answer this question, then you probably aren't ready to retire.

You should have a good understanding of annual expenses, but now you need to think about what you are going to be doing with your time. Specifically, what are you going to be doing during the day, Monday–Friday? Don't think that you need to know exactly what you will be doing; that is bound to change, but you should be able to map out a rough framework of a "normal" retirement day. My advice: use vacation days to test out your retirement life. This is not about "not working." There needs to be a life that you are retiring to, and it needs to be consistent with your values. If you think you'll be doing something the rest of your life, try it now to see what it's like.

Financial freedom allows you to live life without being dependent on income from a job. If you have a personally fulfilling job and are able to live the life that you desire, congrats! If it is personally fulfilling but is commanding too much of your time, see if there are ways to offload responsibility or work part-time. At this point, it is not about income; it is about aligning with other values. If you aren't receiving these non-financial benefits from your job or there isn't room for flexibility, then I'd encourage you to move on with your life. Listen to your body. No one knows you better than you.

The Final Hurdle: "One More Year" Syndrome

It can be very hard to voluntarily retire. It requires action on your part and involves staring down the fears that we've talked about. The easiest path is often just to keep working or to keep kicking the can down the road. This is known as "one more year" syndrome. Working an additional year can actually be beneficial for a few reasons, but only if it is based on opportunity, not fear.

1) It will lower your withdrawal rate, which may help with financial anxiety.

2) It will allow you to better plan your retirement life.

3) Your company may offer a voluntary buyout, and you'll be able to take it. This may be luck-based, but you may be able to forecast if this will be offered.

Working one more year looks great financially, but every sacrifice that you make for that career is a bullet to your soul. At this point, you are giving away your time and energy for money that you don't need. Get ready for a constant feeling of "Why am I doing this?" My advice: pick a date six months out in the future as your retirement date and stick to it. Above all, make sure that your partner is on board. Your retirement greatly affects them as well. It will also take time for them to process it.

You are not your job. You are getting paid to do something for someone else. Your employer has you because they need you to do specific tasks. In all likelihood, it's not your work; you're doing someone else's work. If you retire, you may be giving someone else the opportunity they need to succeed. Trust me, your company will be fine without you. Don't mistake a job for an identity. You are your values, not your job. People often find that their values are incongruent with their jobs. Retirement is one way to solve this incongruence. This is the start line, not the finish line. Life is a Western; get out of your cubicle and experience it.

PART II: LIFE AFTER EARLY RETIREMENT

CHAPTER 11
YOU DID IT, YOU RETIRED EARLY – NOW WHAT?

Congrats on your achievement! No one cares. Ok, I'm sorry, that's harsh. It is a major achievement. You have been working for many years, laser-focused on this goal, and want to shout it from the rooftops. Remember when we discussed how it is an internal goal, and our reasons for doing this aren't based on others' opinions? That doesn't change now. You're going to want affirmation, but it's not realistic to expect it to come from other people. Some have walked this path, but remember that it is very rare. I have walked the path. I'll give you kudos. I know what it took to get here. It really is an amazing accomplishment. Congrats. You should be proud of it.

Social Reaction

Other than the immediate and complete disappearance of work stress, one of the first things that you will experience is the social reaction to your early retirement. Without a doubt, the most common initial response that I've received is surprise. Once you make the decision with your family, the first people that you are going to tell are your supervisors and co-workers. They are going to be surprised for a few reasons:

1) They are used to people leaving for other jobs or for older people retiring, but it is likely the first time they've experienced seeing someone voluntarily leave the workforce entirely at your stage and age.

2) They know more about your career than most people and know what you are walking away from, and

3) It's easy for them to draw parallels between themselves and you.

Telling people at work that you are retiring is a hard process. Be honest! They will likely want to know why, and you should be able to give them a concise answer. It's okay to be really happy. I'm not saying that you should be dancing around the office, but it's okay to be happy. Others will expect you to be happy.

They've known you for years; there's no reason to act inauthentically. I said this before, but they will develop a plan to transition your workload. By stepping away, you are likely giving someone else an opportunity to grow their career and succeed. If you truly believe that you are irreplaceable, you will likely be humbled by the lack of requests after you leave. There is a market for your work skills, so other companies may reach out; just don't expect your office to be unable to function without you.

At the heart of the social reaction is the third reason above: people will compare themselves to you. It's human nature. At best, people will genuinely think about what early retirement means to them. At worst, people may get defensive.

Why is he doing this to his family? He's lazy. He's lying. My advice is just to be very thoughtful about how and if you share this information. You don't need to lie about it, but you may not need to introduce it either. I have friends who know, and I have friends who don't know. Co-workers and family will know your situation, but people outside of these environments don't necessarily need to know.

What is Your Identity?

You are not your job. I'll acknowledge that this is a lot easier to say than to fully accept. It's hard not to gravitate to your job as your identity. This is how people viewed you for 40+ hours every week for years. You put it in credit card applications. It's in bold font on your résumé. It was featured prominently in your signature block. People put in years of effort to get their work titles and career status. However, when you get to early retirement, you're over it. There are things that you value more than your job title. It's your values that define who you are, not your job title. You were obviously very good at your job. You wouldn't have made it here in the first place if you weren't, but you need to stop thinking of yourself as that job. That is completely underselling who you are.

People are going to want to define you, and you're going to want to define this for yourself. What is my identity? Stay-at-home dad checks a lot of boxes. I'm now able to spend more time with my son, get him ready for school every day, be there when he gets home, and take him to his activities. Then again, my son isn't a "stay-at-home kid," so that's not really a great description. I'm a retiree. Granted, that doesn't really describe what I'm doing now. I'm Mr. Fix-it and the landscaper around the house; that could be a good one. I was a youth sports head coach for my son's soccer team; that's another angle. Apparently, I'm an author now. Never saw that one coming. Maybe you see where I'm going with this.

It's multi-faceted, and it evolves. So, who am I? It's pretty simple. I'm John.

Ikigai and the Zuzunaga Venn Diagram of Purpose

Ikigai is an ancient Japanese philosophy for identifying and focusing on the virtues and activities that add meaning to one's life. The Venn Diagram of Purpose was developed by Andrés Zuzunaga in 2012. It is similar to the Ikigai perspective, but is primarily focused on occupation. Although this Venn diagram may not exactly represent the concept of Ikigai, I do think that it's a good way to map out what you can do in retirement to align with your values.

The biggest problem with this chart, in general, is that it implies that one needs to make money to live a meaningful life. Well, we're in a position where we don't need to make money, which opens up a world of possibilities. I still think the other concepts apply, but replace "what you can be paid for." with "how you can help." Eliminating "what you can be paid for." is probably the biggest mental hurdle, but it is incredibly freeing. It is extremely rewarding to do something for someone without a monetary return.

The other change is "what the world needs." That seems like an extreme goal that very few people would ever attain. I like to think through this exercise at several different levels. Create one centered on what you need, individually; one for your family's needs; and one for your community. A world impact isn't impossible and may happen at some point. Still, I wouldn't focus on that, especially not until you have a firm grasp on self, family, and community. It's not about chasing purpose; it is about living your values. Your identity is your values. Your purpose is to live these values.

If your retirement dream is to do nothing, then hey, I have no problem with that. The nice thing is that you don't have to do anything. Your time is yours. However, you may find that you receive deeper fulfillment in life by finding ways to contribute and help others.

Like I said before, early retirement is the start line, not the finish line. It can take some time to move on from your past work identity, but there is so much room left in your life for exponential growth. You have the gift that most people will never have: freedom of time and energy. You've likely spent much of your life looking through a financial prism, but it's time to think much, much broader.

CHAPTER 12
EMBARK ON YOUR EDUCATIONAL RENAISSANCE

What mattered most in your career progression was likely depth within a career field. You may have been challenged to broaden your skills as you advanced in your career, but depth has always been a staple of your success. Now is the time to move completely away from depth and fully embrace the vast opportunity of breadth. It's time to become a student again. There are so many more levels to your brain than just your area of expertise. In my career, I felt like I was living in mental purgatory. Welcome to cognitive freedom. It's time to embark on your educational renaissance.

Where to Start?

With such an immense amount of available information, it's hard to know where to start. I'll admit, this can be intimidating. My advice is to first go to your local library and just walk around. If something interests you, grab it. It doesn't matter if you have a stack of ten books or if you're naturally drawn to topics that you're already knowledgeable about (cough, personal finance, cough); what's most important is that you start reading. After a while, you'll eventually want to branch out into other topics. The first book that helped launch me on this journey was *Investing: The Last Liberal Art,* by Robert G. Hagstrom.

This book discusses the big ideas across multiple disciplines. It is a great starting point before jumping deeper into each field. It covers physics, biology, sociology, psychology, philosophy, literature, mathematics, and decision making. It conveys the importance of building a “latticework” of multi-disciplinary knowledge. Each core component is endlessly fascinating on its own. Still, when you combine them together, it will completely change how you view, well, everything. After learning the basic principles, I’d recommend diving deeper into each of these fields. He does relate the components to investing, but we’re good on that front; we don’t need to change how we invest.

The next book, which opened up new ways of thinking, was *The New Smart: How Nurturing Creativity Will Help Children Thrive*, by Terry Roberts, PhD. This book utilizes Howard Gardner’s Theory of Multiple Intelligences: Linguistic-Verbal, Musical, Logical-Mathematical, Visual-Spatial, Bodily-Kinesthetic, Interpersonal, Intrapersonal, Naturalist, and Existential. It discusses the importance of intertwining these together and gives examples of how to blend them in the school curriculum.

It describes the many failings behind IQ scores and standardized tests, with the key takeaway that intelligence is not one static number, but instead an ever-evolving skillset of adaptability, resilience, and creativity through a combination of different intelligences. The good news is that all of these intelligences can be nurtured and improved. There’s no reason why we can’t apply this to our own lives.

By reaching financial freedom, you are most likely very skilled in Logical-Mathematical, but have room for growth in Linguistic-Verbal (*Hey, I’m trying my best here*), Musical, Visual-Spatial, Bodily-Kinesthetic, Interpersonal, Intrapersonal, Naturalist, and or Existential. By thinking about intelligence through this lens, you'll also have a much greater appreciation when you see people who excel in these different areas.

Beware of Confirmation Bias

Our goal on this educational journey is growth. It can be hard to process new information after you've fallen into a specific way of thinking for so long. Still, you must be open to learning. You will likely get defensive about some things that you read because they challenge your current way of thinking. This is natural. What's important is to recognize when you're acting defensively and think about why. It's okay to be critical and disagree, but think about why. You'll know that the growth process is working when you read something and it feels scratchy. I can't think of a better way to describe it. It's your brain thinking deeply about the material and trying to process a new way of thinking. Take breaks to process the information. It's not a race; there is a lot out there.

Throughout the process, it's important to beware of confirmation bias, which is the tendency to only search for information that confirms pre-existing beliefs. Don't get me wrong, I fall into this trap as well. It can feel really good to view things that you already agree with, but that's not growth. The goal is gaining new knowledge, not seeking confirmation. It can be hard to break out of this spell; that's why it's important to eventually venture out of the personal finance section, be mindful about the type of content that you're viewing, and challenge yourself to seek out new information and perspectives.

CHAPTER 13
SEEING THE WORLD DIFFERENTLY

With your newfound knowledge and perspective, you're going to start seeing the world differently. You're going to feel more like an observer and less like a participant. Get ready for your brain to rewire. You will start to see how things work from a completely different perspective. You're going to need to make sense of what you've learned.

Crystallizing Your Knowledge

Your brain is working like never before, you've gained brand new perspectives, and you're going to want to talk about it. What should you do? Find a group to talk about it! Talk with your friends and family about the new concepts and connections that you've made. You can also do this through online communities. You'll find that the act of communicating forces you to better think through and understand the material. What is most important is being open to feedback and different perspectives.

Another valuable tool in the learning process is writing. Writing forces you to crystallize your thoughts and communicate succinctly. It acts as a way to de-clutter your thoughts and provide more clarity. Writing forces internal connections and requires that you put yourself in the audience's shoes to think about how they would interpret your written message. You will have a flurry of different ideas, but you won't have fully thought them through until you write them down.

The other positive to writing is that it enables your brain to move on to something else. If you have an insightful thought, your brain will do everything it can to hold on to it. This requires mental energy and inhibits new ideas. Writing it down archives the information and allows your brain to move on. The Notes function on your phone is an easy way to quickly capture these ideas, wherever you may be. I had a lot of fun writing this book. It was exhausting, but it was also freeing. With each chapter I wrote, I was able to let go of information and free up mental space for new pursuits.

Human Behavior as a Product of Environment

As an observer, you will be able to easily recognize how human behavior is impacted by things like work, politics, and economics. You'll see how people are heavily influenced by their environments and understand why they act in a certain manner. Incentives often drive behavior. We're not immune to this either; financial freedom drove our past behavior. At the end of the day, we're all just trying to make sense of everything. No one really knows what they're doing. Common values emerge, such as the importance of family and being a part of a community. Still, environmental stressors are often a large detriment to human behavior.

This context should help you with forgiveness and letting go of personal grudges. If you're harboring resentment towards someone, you're probably giving them too much credit. People are products of the stressors of their environments. Humans are emotional. People have bad days. It doesn't make sense to view their actions as fully thought through. Keep in mind that no one really knows what they're doing. People are all trying to make sense of this crazy world.

Show Appreciation

Most people are struggling. They are subjected to far more stressors than is natural and are routinely pushed to their limits. Show them appreciation! Retirement has given me a new perspective on the economic system, and I am in genuine awe when someone uses their energy to help me. My child's teachers, mail carriers, grocery store clerks, garbage collectors, doctors, etc. Occupation doesn't matter; at the end of the day, we're all just people. Not only are these people helping you, but they are likely doing the best that they can with their limited energy. Tell them, thank you! Frequently. As often as you can. Be nice. Show genuine appreciation for others, understand their situations, and don't hold them to unrealistic standards. It doesn't have to be big. Be friendly. Say hi to others. Smile. They will smile back. With zero effort, you just made their day a little brighter.

CHAPTER 14
HELPING OTHERS

You are in an extremely unique situation where you have time, energy, knowledge, and money. Many have none of these things. You are going to want to help people. It's not motivated by guilt, but rather opportunity, and perhaps even a sense of obligation to give back. Helping Others is a revised quadrant of Zuzunaga's Venn Diagram of Purpose that will consist of extremely fulfilling behavior, both for you and for others. How can you help others? Generally, through knowledge, labor, and money.

Knowledge

I can say without a shadow of doubt that you have exceptional knowledge in at least two areas: your previous occupation and, since you made it here, personal finance. You have the ability to impact the lives of others by sharing your knowledge. You have a lot of it, and you're going to want to share it. There are so many different ways to do this. It can be done formally through tutoring, mentoring, presentations, part-time teaching, or writing. It can also be as simple as conversing with friends and family. If you have children, it will be important to teach them about the basics of personal finance.

Labor

In retirement, you're going to have the time and energy to more readily be able to volunteer your labor for your community. There are undoubtedly an innumerable amount of worthwhile opportunities that could use your help. One volunteering opportunity that I found extremely fulfilling was being a youth sports head coach. Without job obligations, I knew that I would be able to attend every practice and game. I felt a huge responsibility to the kids and parents, and put forth a lot of effort to prepare and put everyone in the best position to grow and succeed. It wasn't just about teaching the kids; it was also about being an example for the parents, should they decide to coach in the future. Specific to Gardner's Theory of Multiple Intelligences, youth sports coaching challenged my interpersonal skills. It was a great opportunity, and I'm glad that I volunteered.

Money

Money is arguably the easiest of the three ways to help, but may be the most difficult if you're pinching pennies. There's no need to pinch pennies at this point! Please don't hoard all of your money. Many great charities are doing extraordinary things for worthwhile causes that could use your financial help. It doesn't have to be huge sums of money, but you can help. I'll go into this later, but you're likely going to end up with more money than you need in retirement. Help people in need!

CHAPTER 15
LIVING A HEALTHIER LIFE

One important consequence of retirement is the opportunity to live a healthier life, both physically and mentally. The brain is constantly changing as it interacts with its environment. Chronic stress, poor health, and a general toxic environment have huge negative ramifications on the brain's ability to process information and think clearly and creatively. Money is nothing if you don't have your health. Living a healthy life is a virtuous cycle. Progress in healthy eating, exercising, or sleeping will, in turn, encourage more healthy habits in the other areas as well. Overall health is made up of many components. I'll identify a few and discuss how retirement allows us to greatly improve our well-being.

Mental Health

The first thing that you'll notice in retirement is the abrupt and complete absence of work stress. No more responsibility for too much work and not enough resources. No more deadlines. No more incongruencies between your values and your job. No commute. No more passive-aggressive emails. No more early mornings and late evenings. No unnecessary travel away from your family. You're officially out of the rat race. It's all gone, immediately.

It's not just about what you lose; what you gain back is your time and energy. Additionally, you may be filled with renewed purpose or at least will be able to dedicate more time and energy to your purpose. You can be authentically yourself, every day, all the time. Seeing the world through a new perspective should make you more appreciative of the efforts of others and will help you with forgiveness.

Physical Health

Stress takes a physical toll on your body. Many of the maladies that our bodies face are a result of stress. Simply removing this stress will improve your physical health. Your sleep will improve. The early morning alarm clock is gone, and you'll be able to align your sleep pattern with your natural cycle. Similar to sleep, you will be able to better listen to your body and rest when needed. You'll no longer have to fight against your body and push through to get something done. No afternoon caffeine shot needed. If you are tired, take a nap. Listen to your body. There's always tomorrow. The need for unhealthy stress-relieving activities vanishes as well.

You will be able to eat better in retirement. There's no need for meals "on the go" or eating out on your lunch break. You now have the opportunity to eat healthy meals at home. By stocking your house with healthy food, you will be more likely to eat healthier, and you will feel better. Additionally, with both time and energy, you will be able to exercise better and more regularly. Even though I used to have time in the evenings and weekends with my family, I was often exhausted. That's gone. I now have way more energy during these critical times.

CHAPTER 16
STRUCTURING A "NORMAL" DAY

Alright, so what does a "normal" day look like in retirement? Although you're forgoing the structure of your job, it is important to create some degree of certainty in an uncertain world. It's also about creating healthy habits and identifying and eliminating unhealthy habits. Structure is an important aspect of life and will help greatly when you determine what you do during traditional work hours in retirement.

It's Ok to Do Nothing

I feel like this needs to be highlighted. Don't feel like you need to be productive every day. The terms "productive" and "busy" have likely been hardwired into your brain as an employee to grind out more work product. Rid these words from your vocabulary. Retirement will change how you view time and opportunity cost. While I was working, it was hard to think about retirement without also thinking about lost income. Now, there's no way I would give away my time for money that I don't need. You don't have to be doing something at all times. Your mind and body need activity, but there's nothing wrong with relaxing. It's okay to do nothing. Listen to your body.

Align Your Day with Your Energy

Before retirement, you likely had no choice but to align your schedule with your employer. More productive in the morning? Too bad. Meetings are set, clients are in town, and a new crisis has just emerged. Able to think more creatively in the afternoon? That's also unfortunate. I need you to crunch through the data in these spreadsheets. Well, that's all in the past. You now have the freedom to plan your day to align with your natural energy. It may sound intimidating, but it will eventually reveal itself. Here's my "normal" weekday:

8am:	Wake up
8am–9am:	Get my son ready for school
9am–11am:	Coffee, breakfast, hobbies
11am–12pm:	Daily hike
12pm–1pm:	Shower, lunch
1pm–5pm:	Read, write, errands, creative projects, hobbies
5pm:	Son returns from school

Admittedly, it's not very impressive. What a disaster of productivity. Luckily, it doesn't need to be! Days vary, but this is just a general framework for what naturally works for me. Find what works for you. You're also going to enjoy the new flexibility. Weekday mornings and evenings used to be hectic. A sick kid, a broken car, or a home maintenance issue used to be a disaster. No longer.

Controlling Your Environment

Whatever we are trying to achieve (health, project, new endeavor), we can help ourselves by creating an environment that nudges us toward success. Want to start reading more? Put a stack of books next to where you normally sit. Want to eat healthier? Stock your house with healthy foods. The hardest part of starting something new is simply starting. Put yourself in an environment where you can succeed, and it may become a part of your daily habit.

Beware of over-consumption of TV and media. Similarly, limit how often you check the news and the markets. I make sure that I only check these once per day, at a maximum, after the markets close. You don't need to follow the 24-hour news cycle. It's mostly junk. The big, important stories will find you.

Hiking and Being Outside

I love my daily hike. Any day that I do that hike is a great day. At its worst, it's a great form of exercise. At its best, it's euphoric. On my hike, I feel connected with nature. Observing nature is a great way to visualize the enduring concepts from a variety of disciplines. Equilibrium, exponentiality, herd mentality, adaptability, and compounding are all easily identified by observing the natural world. It also helps me see how everything is connected.

Hiking clears my head and provides a sense of adventure. My thoughts often just come to me when I'm hiking. Much of the content for this book came from thoughts that I had while hiking. Whether I want to or not, I generally return from my hike with pages of notes.

I try to be outside as much as possible. I can't completely explain it, but it feels so much better to be outside. The warmth of the sun. The smell of fresh air. Another activity that I love is landscaping. It combines the positive benefits of manual labor with the freedom of being outside. Taking on big jobs does provide some humbling perspective, however. I have a greater appreciation for people who do that as a job every day. Pretty amazing.

Time Flies By

Time flies by like never before in retirement. I routinely forget which day and even which month it is. It's amazing that since time is no longer a constraint, I hardly pay attention to it. I'm not looking at the clock, and I don't find myself waiting for anything. I'm generally surprised when my afternoon alarm goes off to tell me that my son's school bus is arriving. I'm in a flow state far more frequently than before. Do I ever get bored? Sure, at times. However, I'm much less bored now than I used to be.

CHAPTER 17
ADVENTURE OVER RELAXATION

You might view retirement as a time for relaxation, but that's not really what it's about. There is definitely time for relaxation, but what's much more compelling is adventure. Adventure is about trying new things, going to new places, meeting new people, and challenging yourself to think differently. Exploring the world and your own mind. Adventure requires vulnerability. Things will not go as you plan. It requires adaptability. It requires being open-minded, not anchoring on your past beliefs. It requires resilience. The only constant in life is change. Uncertainty is a feature of life, not a bug. Embrace it!

The Power of Travel

Travel is an amazing form of adventure. Within a day's worth of travel, you can reach almost anywhere in the world. It's really incredible when you stop and think about it. No matter where we go, traveling requires our brains to learn. Even in the weeks preceding a trip, our brains are filled with new activity. New adventures, new food, new cultures, new natural landscapes, all there to be explored and experienced. It's okay if things don't go as planned.

These are the moments that become even more memorable. The benefits don't end when the travel ends either. When you return to your "normal" life, you have brand new perspectives and memories that will last a lifetime. No, you don't need to fly privately or sit in first class to experience the benefits of travel. Relaxing on the beach is nice, I can't argue against that, but I'm much more drawn to new adventures. Without constant work stress, I no longer feel a need to vacation to escape or for stress relief. It's all about adventure.

Trying New Things

Fortunately, we don't have to travel to experience adventure. It's all around us, even at home and in our local communities. Any new activity can be viewed as an adventure. Challenge yourself in areas where you feel deficient. If it doesn't catch on, so what? If something seems too intimidating, you should just try it. Who cares if you "fail." You'll learn something about the subject and about yourself. I think you're going to be surprised by how often you succeed and the fulfillment that it brings. This also produces a virtuous cycle where you will have more confidence that you can succeed in other pursuits.

CHAPTER 18
HAVE FUN!

Above all, remember to have fun. You may have been too future-focused prior to financial freedom; now it's time to learn to enjoy the present. Enjoy your freedom and what you have accomplished. Very few people make it here. The definition of fun will vary for each person. I'd argue that most people don't experience fun as often as they should. It's almost as though people don't allow themselves to have fun. How absurd!

Embrace Your Hobbies

If it's interesting, pursue it! If it provides enjoyment, delve deeper! Feel free to fully enjoy your hobbies. It's your time; you can decide how you spend it. Find your joy and don't worry about others' definition of joy. All hobbies could be considered "dumb"; don't worry about it, don't apologize for it. Be authentically you. It doesn't have to sound exciting, either. Some hobbies that I've personally listed are reading, writing, and hiking. I'll touch on this in the next chapter, but amazingly, these are all inexpensive.

It's important to regularly exercise your mind and your body in retirement. Hobbies provide us with the opportunity to do both of these things, often simultaneously. Additionally, it can be important to find a community of people who have similar interests and interact with them as well. There are many hobbies that you can enjoy by yourself, but discussing them with other people can provide even more fulfillment. There's no telling where those new connections may lead.

At the end of the day, we're just tiny specs of stardust living in an explosively vast universe over a minuscule time period of life. Don't take your life too seriously. Please, please, please, remember to have fun!

CHAPTER 19
MANAGING FINANCES IN RETIREMENT

Begrudgingly, it's time to talk about money again. By this point, you should see that living in retirement is not about money. It was certainly important pre-retirement because it does allow you to get to this point, but now it's not really a large focus. You did it; you're set for life as long as you don't screw it up. Regardless, let's take a dive into how your perspective on finances changes in retirement.

The Focus Shifts to Tax Efficiency

In retirement, expenses are taxed. It sounds weird to say, but hear me out. Outside of dividends and interest, you will be able to control your income, which will be determined by your expenses. The higher the expenses, the more you will have to withdraw, which may impact your tax bracket. So what's the best withdrawal strategy? Start with cash and selling stocks from your brokerage account. Turning off automatic dividend reinvestment will help replenish some of your cash balance every year. If you need to pull from retirement accounts, you can set up a SEPP or Roth conversion ladder. You can withdraw Roth contributions penalty-free if you need to.

The focus on how to withdraw generally comes down to tax efficiency. Many of the financial tools are about deferring taxes. That doesn't mean that you don't have to pay at some point. You do have to pay. The IRS knows what they're doing. You're not going to get around paying taxes. The two constants in life are death and taxes. Accept it.

However, since tax rates vary by source and income level, it is possible to combine withdrawals from different accounts to minimize your tax burden. Software exists to do this for you, but there is one general topic that we can discuss: Required Minimum Distributions (RMDs).

The IRS requires you to liquidate a certain percentage of your deferred tax accounts every year starting in your mid-70s. You don't have to spend all of the money; you can just put it into your brokerage account with other after-tax dollars. The issue is that the forced selling through RMDs can create large taxable events. There is a way to mitigate this impact: Roth conversions. Instead of having large forced taxable events in your 70s, you can start doing it now, when your income is lower, by converting some of your traditional funds to Roth every year.

We already covered the benefits of Roth accounts in Part I of this book. If you can convert your money to a Roth at a reasonable tax rate, do it. Roth conversions greatly benefit early retirees because you're able to stretch out the conversions over more years. Keep in mind that you will pay tax in the year that the money is converted to Roth. Do you need a financial advisor? No. Why change what worked? If you desire, there is software available that can calculate the impacts of Roth conversions and recommend a withdrawal strategy.

State taxes should be taken into account, but I would not move somewhere just for tax purposes. Live where you want to live. This is about lifestyle, not about money. If you are convinced that you want to live in a state with low income taxes, at least take all taxes into account: property, sales, etc.

States need tax dollars to provide services for residents. If it doesn't come from income, it has to come from somewhere else. Keep that in mind.

You're Going to Have More Money Than You Need

It is common for retirees who are knowledgeable about personal finance to underspend in retirement. For starters, the 4% rule is inherently conservative and is based on historical worst-case scenarios. It assumes a static withdrawal amount (adjusted for inflation). If a massive drop occurs in the market, you don't have to withdraw that set amount. Also, as we discussed for sequence of returns risk, you can withdraw from your cash account and leave your stock accounts untouched.

Additionally, the 4% rule assumes no additional income. We haven't even addressed income from Social Security. If you really need additional income, I have no doubts that you could easily figure out a way to use your talents.

Finally, expenses often drop in retirement. Expenses for commuting, parking, dry cleaning, eating out for meals, and stress-reducing vices all disappear. Also, your mortgage will eventually be paid off, further reducing your expenses. I mentioned that my three most common daily activities are hiking, reading, and writing. All inexpensive. Even with all of these things considered, many retirees will be even more conservative and try to stay below the 4% safe withdrawal rate. It can be hard to change your ingrained attitude toward expenses, but it is okay to ease off at this point.

Your Money is Not Your Legacy

In retirement, you're going to think about your legacy. What are you leaving behind? How will you be remembered? Your legacy isn't your money. Your legacy is your values, and it lives on through the people you've interacted with. Legacy isn't a dollar value; it's a collection of the memorable impacts that other people will have of you. If you get nothing else from this book, while you are here on this Earth, use your time, money, and energy on the things that you like and the people that you love.

CHAPTER 20
LIFE IS A WESTERN

Western films are characterized by new beginnings, individualism, adventure, resilience, and brash optimism in the face of an ever-changing, uncertain world. Life is a Western. You cannot shake my optimism. The winds are always shifting, and the rules of the game are constantly changing, but those who can properly adapt and stay true to their values have the greatest chance of success.

"To become good at anything, you have to know how to apply basic principles. To become great at it, you have to know when to violate those principles."

— Garry Kasparov, *Deep Thinking: Where Machine Intelligence Ends and Human Creativity Begins*

The Unknown Frontier

Anyone who says they know with certainty what will happen in the future is lying. No one knows. Education and experience don't necessarily make you feel better about something. Still, it can make you more prepared for what may occur. What matters is adaptability and resilience. The unexpected will occur. How will you respond? You don't have to have everything figured out on this journey. In fact, you never will. No matter what, there will always be a boogeyman. Stay true to your values and help others along the way. Stay humble and be thankful for what you have. This level of freedom is extremely rare. And for the last time, go outside!

AFTERWORD

Early retirees are more lost than you might think. I found that although much of the material on the market is about achieving financial freedom, there is very little about living in early retirement. Retirement requires a major shift in mindset: asset accumulation to protection and liquidation, depth to breadth, time scarcity to time abundance, energy utilization motivation from external to internal, long-term goal focus to new adventures, forced work community to self-nurtured relationships, forced daily schedule to self-directed, productivity focus to undefined work, and built-in excuses to no excuses.

I tried to minimize numbers and equations throughout this book. That material is widespread. This book isn't about numbers and portfolio allocation; it's about living your best life. Only one number matters: your early retirement number. The compound interest equation was included to show the impact of time, but also to induce exponential thinking. This book isn't perfect, but that's part of the point. You don't have to be perfect, and you don't have to know everything.

There's no reason why you can't discover the breadth discussed in Part II during your working years, theoretically. Still, you are likely fighting against others demanding your time and energy. It isn't just about time; it's the suffocation of energy. I didn't go too deeply into the books that I've referenced because I want you to read them. Please, read those books. Keep reading and discovering.

If you like this book, please review it on Goodreads and Amazon.

ACKNOWLEDGEMENTS

My absolute, deepest thank you to the following individuals. Without your insights, support, and lasting influence, this book could never have been written.

My wife, Jessica. A strong, beautiful, independent woman. You are the smartest person that I know. Thank you for being so understanding as I embarked into the unknown world of early retirement. I still don't know how you've put up with me after all of these years.

My son, Jacob. You are the reason why I jump out of bed every morning. My perspective on life's priorities completely changed when you were born. Spending time with you and watching you grow as a person brings me unfathomably deep fulfillment.

My Mom. Thank you for pushing me to challenge myself in my formative years and for always being a pillar of support in my life.

My Dad. Thank you for teaching me Microsoft Excel basics at a young age, discussing the idea of pursuing a retirement number, and modeling a retirement life.

My wife's parents, Peter and Kathy. Thank you for modeling a fantastic retirement life and making me think about how I could spend my time in retirement.

Everyone who had to deal with me at the end of my career. I know that my attitude was deteriorating near the end, and it was time for me to move on. Thanks for bearing with me!

Connor and the OTR community. Thank you to my friends in the best online "dive bar in northern Wisconsin" for your honest and ever-interesting perspectives on Big Ten sports, politics, parenting, books, movies, album reviews (so many album reviews), and most of all, life.

Everyone in the FIRE community and the pioneers who piloted the process. Thank you for outlining the process, showing that early retirement is actually possible, and for understanding why I referred to it as financial freedom instead of financial independence. Sorry! (FFRE?)

www.ingramcontent.com/pod-product-compliance
Lightning Source LLC
LaVergne TN
LVHW020237210926
848481LV00016B/2350
* 9 7 9 8 9 9 5 4 9 0 5 1 7 *